16.49

D1274716

WITHDRAWN

Little
Pebble™

Colorful Foods

# Yellow Foods

by Martha E. H. Rustad

CAPSTONE PRESS
a capstone imprint

Little Pebble is published by Capstone Press,
1710 Roe Crest Drive, North Mankato, Minnesota 56003
www.mycapstone.com

**Library of Congress Cataloging-in-Publication Data**
Names: Rustad, Martha E. H. (Martha Elizabeth Hillman), 1975– author.
Title: Yellow foods / by Martha E. H. Rustad.
Description: North Mankato, Minnesota : Capstone Press, [2017] | Audience: Ages 4–7. | Audience: K to grade 3. | Includes bibliographical references and index.
Identifiers: LCCN 2016009742| ISBN 9781515723714 (library binding) | ISBN 9781515723752 (pbk.) | ISBN 9781515723790 (ebook (pdf)
Subjects: LCSH: Food—Juvenile literature. | Yellow—Juvenile literature. | Color of food—Juvenile literature.
Classification: LCC TX355 .R857 2017 | DDC 641.3—dc23
LC record available at http://lccn.loc.gov/2016009742

**Editorial Credits**
Megan Atwood, editor; Juliette Peters, designer;
Jo Miller, media researcher; Steve Walker, production specialist

**Photo Credits**
Images by Capstone Studio: Karon Dubke
Photo styling: Sarah Schuette and Marcy Morin

Printed and bound in China

PO007712LEOF16

# Table of Contents

# Yellow Foods

Have you ever tasted

the color yellow?

Let's think of yellow foods.

# Yellow Fruits

Eat a yellow banana.

It is a healthy snack.

Pineapples take six
months to grow.
They taste sweet and tart.

Mangoes grow on trees.

They are yellow and juicy.

Lemonade tastes sweet.

Slurp!

It is made from lemons.

# Yellow Vegetables

Corn grows tall.

Eat it off the cob.

Summer squash grows
in a garden.

It turns yellow when ripe.

# Yellow Meals

Dad makes eggs.

We eat them before school.

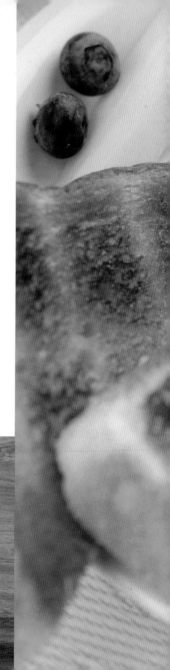

My aunt makes yellow curry.

It is good with rice.

What other foods are yellow?

# Glossary

**cob**—the middle part of an ear of corn

**curry**—a dish cooked in strong spices; many curry dishes come from India and Thailand

**ripe**—ready to be picked and eaten

**squash**—a vegetable that grows on a bush with many vines; summer squashes are ripe in the summer

# Read More

Adamson, Heather. *Yellow*. Colors in Nature. Minneapolis: Bullfrog Books, 2014.

Nunn, Daniel. *Yellow*. Colors All Around Us. Chicago: Heinemann-Raintree, 2012.

Stevens, Madeline. *Yellow Around Me*. Color in My World. New York: Cavendish Square, 2015.

# Internet Sites

FactHound offers a safe, fun way to find Internet sites related to this book. All of the sites on FactHound have been researched by our staff.

Here's all you do:
Visit *www.facthound.com*
Type in this code: 9781515723714

# Index